TODAY I POOPED!

DATE: 15/6 1.

LOCATION:

L

WHY THIS LOCATION

that's where I were

CHARACTERISTICS

Sludgy

SETTING

CONCLUSION

Yuk

RECOMMENDATION

Sew up bum hole!

RATING: ___/5 STARS

TODAY I POOPED!

DATE: 16/5/19

LOCATION:

En Suite

WHY THIS LOCATION

woke up at 3am
for a pee & a poop came out!

CHARACTERISTICS

Firm

SETTING

CONCLUSION

RECOMMENDATION

RATING: ___/5 STARS

TODAY I POOPED!

DATE: 18/5/19

LOCATION: En Suite

WHY THIS LOCATION
Didn't want to stink our downstairs!

CHARACTERISTICS
firm

SETTING

CONCLUSION
doing everything right

RECOMMENDATION

RATING: __/5 STARS

TODAY I POOPED!

DATE: 19|5|19

LOCATION:
En suite   2.30am

WHY THIS LOCATION   was asleep

CHARACTERISTICS   almost runny

SETTING

CONCLUSION

RECOMMENDATION

RATING: ___/5 STARS

TODAY I POOPED!

DATE: 21/5/19

LOCATION: En Suite 11pm

WHY THIS LOCATION: didn't want to stink up downstairs

CHARACTERISTICS: firm but with white mucus.

SETTING:

CONCLUSION:

RECOMMENDATION:

RATING: ___/5 STARS

TODAY I POOPED!

DATE:

LOCATION:

WHY THIS LOCATION

CHARACTERISTICS

SETTING

CONCLUSION

RECOMMENDATION

RATING: ___/5 STARS

TODAY I POOPED!

DATE:

LOCATION:

WHY THIS LOCATION

CHARACTERISTICS

SETTING

CONCLUSION

RECOMMENDATION

RATING: ___/5 STARS

TODAY I POOPED!

DATE:

LOCATION:

WHY THIS LOCATION

CHARACTERISTICS

SETTING

CONCLUSION

RECOMMENDATION

RATING: ___/5 STARS

TODAY I POOPED!

DATE:

LOCATION:

WHY THIS LOCATION

CHARACTERISTICS

SETTING

CONCLUSION

RECOMMENDATION

RATING: ___/5 STARS

TODAY I POOPED!

DATE:

LOCATION:

WHY THIS LOCATION

CHARACTERISTICS

SETTING

CONCLUSION

RECOMMENDATION

RATING: ___/5 STARS

TODAY I POOPED!

DATE:

LOCATION:

WHY THIS LOCATION

CHARACTERISTICS

SETTING

CONCLUSION

RECOMMENDATION

RATING: __/5 STARS

TODAY I POOPED!

DATE:

LOCATION:

WHY THIS LOCATION

CHARACTERISTICS

SETTING

CONCLUSION

RECOMMENDATION

RATING: __/5 STARS

TODAY I POOPED!

DATE:

LOCATION:

WHY THIS LOCATION

CHARACTERISTICS

SETTING

CONCLUSION

RECOMMENDATION

RATING: ___/5 STARS

TODAY I POOPED!

DATE:

LOCATION:

WHY THIS LOCATION

CHARACTERISTICS

SETTING

CONCLUSION

RECOMMENDATION

RATING: ___/5 STARS

TODAY I POOPED!

DATE:

LOCATION:

WHY THIS LOCATION

CHARACTERISTICS

SETTING

CONCLUSION

RECOMMENDATION

RATING: ___/5 STARS

TODAY I POOPED!

DATE:

LOCATION:

WHY THIS LOCATION

CHARACTERISTICS

SETTING

CONCLUSION

RECOMMENDATION

RATING: ___/5 STARS

TODAY I POOPED!

DATE:

LOCATION:

WHY THIS LOCATION

CHARACTERISTICS

SETTING

CONCLUSION

RECOMMENDATION

RATING: ___/5 STARS

TODAY I POOPED!

DATE:

LOCATION:

WHY THIS LOCATION

CHARACTERISTICS

SETTING

CONCLUSION

RECOMMENDATION

RATING: ___/5 STARS

TODAY I POOPED!

DATE:

LOCATION:

WHY THIS LOCATION

CHARACTERISTICS

SETTING

CONCLUSION

RECOMMENDATION

RATING: ___/5 STARS

TODAY I POOPED!

DATE:

LOCATION:

WHY THIS LOCATION

CHARACTERISTICS

SETTING

CONCLUSION

RECOMMENDATION

RATING: __/5 STARS

TODAY I POOPED!

DATE:

LOCATION:

WHY THIS LOCATION

CHARACTERISTICS

SETTING

CONCLUSION

RECOMMENDATION

RATING: __/5 STARS

TODAY I POOPED!

DATE:

LOCATION:

WHY THIS LOCATION

CHARACTERISTICS

SETTING

CONCLUSION

RECOMMENDATION

RATING: ___/5 STARS

TODAY I POOPED!

DATE:

LOCATION:

WHY THIS LOCATION

CHARACTERISTICS

SETTING

CONCLUSION

RECOMMENDATION

RATING: __/5 STARS

TODAY I POOPED!

DATE:

LOCATION:

WHY THIS LOCATION

CHARACTERISTICS

SETTING

CONCLUSION

RECOMMENDATION

RATING: ___/5 STARS

TODAY I POOPED!

DATE:

LOCATION:

WHY THIS LOCATION

CHARACTERISTICS

SETTING

CONCLUSION

RECOMMENDATION

RATING: ___/5 STARS

TODAY I POOPED!

DATE:

LOCATION:

WHY THIS LOCATION

CHARACTERISTICS

SETTING

CONCLUSION

RECOMMENDATION

RATING: ___/5 STARS

TODAY I POOPED!

DATE:

LOCATION:

WHY THIS LOCATION

CHARACTERISTICS

SETTING

CONCLUSION

RECOMMENDATION

RATING: ___/5 STARS

TODAY I POOPED!

DATE:

LOCATION:

WHY THIS LOCATION

CHARACTERISTICS

SETTING

CONCLUSION

RECOMMENDATION

RATING: __/5 STARS

TODAY I POOPED!

DATE:

LOCATION:

WHY THIS LOCATION

CHARACTERISTICS

SETTING

CONCLUSION

RECOMMENDATION

RATING: ___/5 STARS

TODAY I POOPED!

DATE:

LOCATION:

WHY THIS LOCATION

CHARACTERISTICS

SETTING

CONCLUSION

RECOMMENDATION

RATING: ___/5 STARS

TODAY I POOPED!

DATE:

LOCATION:

WHY THIS LOCATION

CHARACTERISTICS

SETTING

CONCLUSION

RECOMMENDATION

RATING: __/5 STARS

TODAY I POOPED!

DATE:

LOCATION:

WHY THIS LOCATION

CHARACTERISTICS

SETTING

CONCLUSION

RECOMMENDATION

RATING: ___/5 STARS

TODAY I POOPED!

DATE:

LOCATION:

WHY THIS LOCATION

CHARACTERISTICS

SETTING

CONCLUSION

RECOMMENDATION

RATING: ___/5 STARS

TODAY I POOPED!

DATE:

LOCATION:

WHY THIS LOCATION

CHARACTERISTICS

SETTING

CONCLUSION

RECOMMENDATION

RATING: ___/5 STARS

TODAY I POOPED!

DATE:

LOCATION:

WHY THIS LOCATION

CHARACTERISTICS

SETTING

CONCLUSION

RECOMMENDATION

RATING: ___/5 STARS

TODAY I POOPED!

DATE:

LOCATION:

WHY THIS LOCATION

CHARACTERISTICS

SETTING

CONCLUSION

RECOMMENDATION

RATING: ___/5 STARS

TODAY I POOPED!

DATE:

LOCATION:

WHY THIS LOCATION

CHARACTERISTICS

SETTING

CONCLUSION

RECOMMENDATION

RATING: ___/5 STARS

TODAY I POOPED!

DATE:

LOCATION:

WHY THIS LOCATION

CHARACTERISTICS

SETTING

CONCLUSION

RECOMMENDATION

RATING: ___/5 STARS

TODAY I POOPED!

DATE:

LOCATION:

WHY THIS LOCATION

CHARACTERISTICS

SETTING

CONCLUSION

RECOMMENDATION

RATING: ___/5 STARS

TODAY I POOPED!

DATE:

LOCATION:

WHY THIS LOCATION

CHARACTERISTICS

SETTING

CONCLUSION

RECOMMENDATION

RATING: ___/5 STARS

TODAY I POOPED!

DATE:

LOCATION:

WHY THIS LOCATION

CHARACTERISTICS

SETTING

CONCLUSION

RECOMMENDATION

RATING: __/5 STARS

TODAY I POOPED!

DATE:

LOCATION:

WHY THIS LOCATION

CHARACTERISTICS

SETTING

CONCLUSION

RECOMMENDATION

RATING: ___/5 STARS

TODAY I POOPED!

DATE:

LOCATION:

WHY THIS LOCATION

CHARACTERISTICS

SETTING

CONCLUSION

RECOMMENDATION

RATING: __/5 STARS

TODAY I POOPED!

DATE:

LOCATION:

WHY THIS LOCATION

CHARACTERISTICS

SETTING

CONCLUSION

RECOMMENDATION

RATING: ___/5 STARS

TODAY I POOPED!

DATE:

LOCATION:

WHY THIS LOCATION

CHARACTERISTICS

SETTING

CONCLUSION

RECOMMENDATION

RATING: ___/5 STARS

TODAY I POOPED!

DATE:

LOCATION:

WHY THIS LOCATION

CHARACTERISTICS

SETTING

CONCLUSION

RECOMMENDATION

RATING: ___/5 STARS

TODAY I POOPED!

DATE:

LOCATION:

WHY THIS LOCATION

CHARACTERISTICS

SETTING

CONCLUSION

RECOMMENDATION

RATING: ___/5 STARS

TODAY I POOPED!

DATE:

LOCATION:

WHY THIS LOCATION

CHARACTERISTICS

SETTING

CONCLUSION

RECOMMENDATION

RATING: ___/5 STARS

TODAY I POOPED!

DATE:

LOCATION:

WHY THIS LOCATION

CHARACTERISTICS

SETTING

CONCLUSION

RECOMMENDATION

RATING: ___/5 STARS

TODAY I POOPED!

DATE:

LOCATION:

WHY THIS LOCATION

CHARACTERISTICS

SETTING

CONCLUSION

RECOMMENDATION

RATING: ___/5 STARS

TODAY I POOPED!

DATE:

LOCATION:

WHY THIS LOCATION

CHARACTERISTICS

SETTING

CONCLUSION

RECOMMENDATION

RATING: __/5 STARS

TODAY I POOPED!

DATE:

LOCATION:

WHY THIS LOCATION

CHARACTERISTICS

SETTING

CONCLUSION

RECOMMENDATION

RATING: __/5 STARS

TODAY I POOPED!

DATE:

LOCATION:

WHY THIS LOCATION

CHARACTERISTICS

SETTING

CONCLUSION

RECOMMENDATION

RATING: __/5 STARS

TODAY I POOPED!

DATE:

LOCATION:

WHY THIS LOCATION

CHARACTERISTICS

SETTING

CONCLUSION

RECOMMENDATION

RATING: ___/5 STARS

TODAY I POOPED!

DATE:

LOCATION:

WHY THIS LOCATION

CHARACTERISTICS

SETTING

CONCLUSION

RECOMMENDATION

RATING: ___/5 STARS

TODAY I POOPED!

DATE:

LOCATION:

WHY THIS LOCATION

CHARACTERISTICS

SETTING

CONCLUSION

RECOMMENDATION

RATING: ___/5 STARS

TODAY I POOPED!

DATE:

LOCATION:

WHY THIS LOCATION

CHARACTERISTICS

SETTING

CONCLUSION

RECOMMENDATION

RATING: ___/5 STARS

TODAY I POOPED!

DATE:

LOCATION:

WHY THIS LOCATION

CHARACTERISTICS

SETTING

CONCLUSION

RECOMMENDATION

RATING: ___/5 STARS

TODAY I POOPED!

DATE:

LOCATION:

WHY THIS LOCATION

CHARACTERISTICS

SETTING

CONCLUSION

RECOMMENDATION

RATING: ___/5 STARS

TODAY I POOPED!

DATE:

LOCATION:

WHY THIS LOCATION

CHARACTERISTICS

SETTING

CONCLUSION

RECOMMENDATION

RATING: __/5 STARS

TODAY I POOPED!

DATE:

LOCATION:

WHY THIS LOCATION

CHARACTERISTICS

SETTING

CONCLUSION

RECOMMENDATION

RATING: ___/5 STARS

TODAY I POOPED!

DATE:

LOCATION:

WHY THIS LOCATION

CHARACTERISTICS

SETTING

CONCLUSION

RECOMMENDATION

RATING: ___/5 STARS

TODAY I POOPED!

DATE:

LOCATION:

WHY THIS LOCATION

CHARACTERISTICS

SETTING

CONCLUSION

RECOMMENDATION

RATING: ___/5 STARS

TODAY I POOPED!

DATE:

LOCATION:

WHY THIS LOCATION

CHARACTERISTICS

SETTING

CONCLUSION

RECOMMENDATION

RATING: __ /5 STARS

TODAY I POOPED!

DATE:

LOCATION:

WHY THIS LOCATION

CHARACTERISTICS

SETTING

CONCLUSION

RECOMMENDATION

RATING: ___/5 STARS

TODAY I POOPED!

DATE:

LOCATION:

WHY THIS LOCATION

CHARACTERISTICS

SETTING

CONCLUSION

RECOMMENDATION

RATING: ___/5 STARS

TODAY I POOPED!

DATE:

LOCATION:

WHY THIS LOCATION

CHARACTERISTICS

SETTING

CONCLUSION

RECOMMENDATION

RATING: ___/5 STARS

TODAY I POOPED!

DATE:

LOCATION:

WHY THIS LOCATION

CHARACTERISTICS

SETTING

CONCLUSION

RECOMMENDATION

RATING: ___/5 STARS

TODAY I POOPED!

DATE:

LOCATION:

WHY THIS LOCATION

CHARACTERISTICS

SETTING

CONCLUSION

RECOMMENDATION

RATING: ___/5 STARS

TODAY I POOPED!

DATE:

LOCATION:

WHY THIS LOCATION

CHARACTERISTICS

SETTING

CONCLUSION

RECOMMENDATION

RATING: ___/5 STARS

TODAY I POOPED!

DATE:

LOCATION:

WHY THIS LOCATION

CHARACTERISTICS

SETTING

CONCLUSION

RECOMMENDATION

RATING: ___/5 STARS

TODAY I POOPED!

DATE:

LOCATION:

WHY THIS LOCATION

CHARACTERISTICS

SETTING

CONCLUSION

RECOMMENDATION

RATING: ___/5 STARS

TODAY I POOPED!

DATE:

LOCATION:

WHY THIS LOCATION

CHARACTERISTICS

SETTING

CONCLUSION

RECOMMENDATION

RATING: ___/5 STARS

TODAY I POOPED!

DATE:

LOCATION:

WHY THIS LOCATION

CHARACTERISTICS

SETTING

CONCLUSION

RECOMMENDATION

RATING: ___/5 STARS

TODAY I POOPED!

DATE:

LOCATION:

WHY THIS LOCATION

CHARACTERISTICS

SETTING

CONCLUSION

RECOMMENDATION

RATING: ___/5 STARS

TODAY I POOPED!

DATE:

LOCATION:

WHY THIS LOCATION

CHARACTERISTICS

SETTING

CONCLUSION

RECOMMENDATION

RATING: ___/5 STARS

TODAY I POOPED!

DATE:

LOCATION:

WHY THIS LOCATION

CHARACTERISTICS

SETTING

CONCLUSION

RECOMMENDATION

RATING: __/5 STARS

TODAY I POOPED!

DATE:

LOCATION:

WHY THIS LOCATION

CHARACTERISTICS

SETTING

CONCLUSION

RECOMMENDATION

RATING: ___/5 STARS

TODAY I POOPED!

DATE:

LOCATION:

WHY THIS LOCATION

CHARACTERISTICS

SETTING

CONCLUSION

RECOMMENDATION

RATING: ___/5 STARS

TODAY I POOPED!

DATE:

LOCATION:

WHY THIS LOCATION

CHARACTERISTICS

SETTING

CONCLUSION

RECOMMENDATION

RATING: ___/5 STARS

TODAY I POOPED!

DATE:

LOCATION:

WHY THIS LOCATION

CHARACTERISTICS

SETTING

CONCLUSION

RECOMMENDATION

RATING: ___/5 STARS

TODAY I POOPED!

DATE:

LOCATION:

WHY THIS LOCATION

CHARACTERISTICS

SETTING

CONCLUSION

RECOMMENDATION

RATING: ___/5 STARS

TODAY I POOPED!

DATE:

LOCATION:

WHY THIS LOCATION

CHARACTERISTICS

SETTING

CONCLUSION

RECOMMENDATION

RATING: __/5 STARS

TODAY I POOPED!

DATE:

LOCATION:

WHY THIS LOCATION

CHARACTERISTICS

SETTING

CONCLUSION

RECOMMENDATION

RATING: ___/5 STARS

TODAY I POOPED!

DATE:

LOCATION:

WHY THIS LOCATION

CHARACTERISTICS

SETTING

CONCLUSION

RECOMMENDATION

RATING: __/5 STARS

TODAY I POOPED!

DATE:

LOCATION:

WHY THIS LOCATION

CHARACTERISTICS

SETTING

CONCLUSION

RECOMMENDATION

RATING: ___/5 STARS

TODAY I POOPED!

DATE:

LOCATION:

WHY THIS LOCATION

CHARACTERISTICS

SETTING

CONCLUSION

RECOMMENDATION

RATING: __/5 STARS

TODAY I POOPED!

DATE:

LOCATION:

WHY THIS LOCATION

CHARACTERISTICS

SETTING

CONCLUSION

RECOMMENDATION

RATING: ___/5 STARS

TODAY I POOPED!

DATE:

LOCATION:

WHY THIS LOCATION

CHARACTERISTICS

SETTING

CONCLUSION

RECOMMENDATION

RATING: ___/5 STARS

TODAY I POOPED!

DATE:

LOCATION:

WHY THIS LOCATION

CHARACTERISTICS

SETTING

CONCLUSION

RECOMMENDATION

RATING: ___/5 STARS

TODAY I POOPED!

DATE:

LOCATION:

WHY THIS LOCATION
_____

CHARACTERISTICS
_____

SETTING
_____

CONCLUSION
_____

RECOMMENDATION
_____

RATING: __/5 STARS

TODAY I POOPED!

DATE:

LOCATION:

WHY THIS LOCATION

CHARACTERISTICS

SETTING

CONCLUSION

RECOMMENDATION

RATING: ___/5 STARS

TODAY I POOPED!

DATE:

LOCATION:

WHY THIS LOCATION

CHARACTERISTICS

SETTING

CONCLUSION

RECOMMENDATION

RATING: __/5 STARS

TODAY I POOPED!

DATE:

LOCATION:

WHY THIS LOCATION

CHARACTERISTICS

SETTING

CONCLUSION

RECOMMENDATION

RATING: __/5 STARS

TODAY I POOPED!

DATE:

LOCATION:

WHY THIS LOCATION

CHARACTERISTICS

SETTING

CONCLUSION

RECOMMENDATION

RATING: ___/5 STARS

TODAY I POOPED!

DATE:

LOCATION:

WHY THIS LOCATION

CHARACTERISTICS

SETTING

CONCLUSION

RECOMMENDATION

RATING: ___/5 STARS

TODAY I POOPED!

DATE:

LOCATION:

WHY THIS LOCATION

CHARACTERISTICS

SETTING

CONCLUSION

RECOMMENDATION

RATING: __/5 STARS

TODAY I POOPED!

DATE:

LOCATION:

WHY THIS LOCATION

CHARACTERISTICS

SETTING

CONCLUSION

RECOMMENDATION

RATING: __/5 STARS

TODAY I POOPED!

DATE:

LOCATION:

WHY THIS LOCATION

CHARACTERISTICS

SETTING

CONCLUSION

RECOMMENDATION

RATING: ___/5 STARS

TODAY I POOPED!

DATE:

LOCATION:

WHY THIS LOCATION

CHARACTERISTICS

SETTING

CONCLUSION

RECOMMENDATION

RATING: ___/5 STARS

Printed in Great Britain
by Amazon